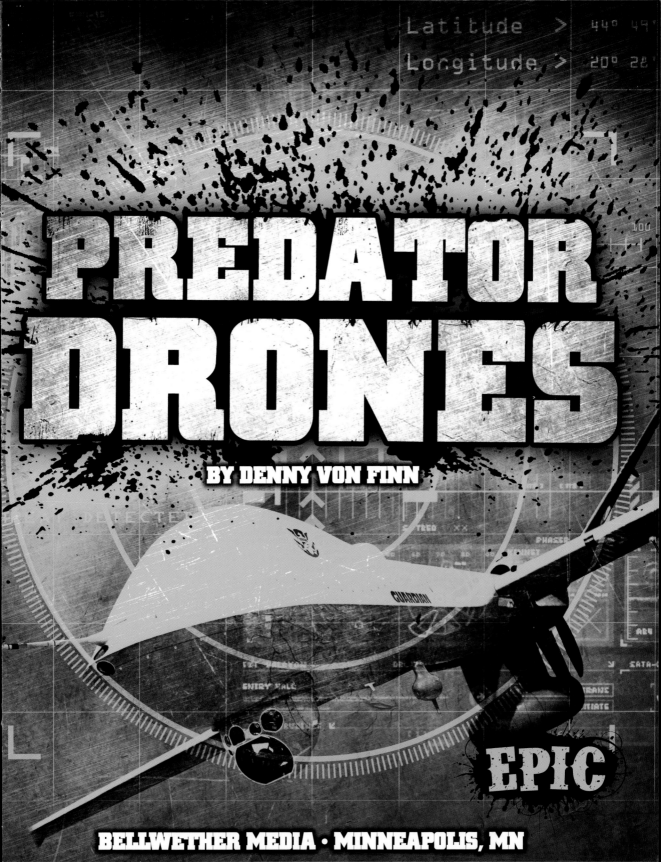

PREDATOR DRONES

BY DENNY VON FINN

BELLWETHER MEDIA · MINNEAPOLIS, MN

EPIC

EPIC BOOKS are no ordinary books. They burst with intense action, high-speed heroics, and shadows of the unknown. Are you ready for an Epic adventure?

This edition first published in 2013 by Bellwether Media, Inc.

No part of this publication may be reproduced in whole or in part without written permission of the publisher. For information regarding permission, write to Bellwether Media, Inc., Attention: Permissions Department, 5357 Penn Avenue South, Minneapolis, MN 55419.

Library of Congress Cataloging-in-Publication Data

Von Finn, Denny.
  Predator drones / by Denny Von Finn.
    p. cm. – (Epic books: military vehicles)
  Includes bibliographical references and index.
  Summary: "Engaging images accompany information about Predator drones. The combination of high-interest subject matter and light text is intended for students in grades 2 through 7"–Provided by publisher.
  Audience: Grades 2-7.
  ISBN 978-1-60014-821-7 (hbk. : alk. paper)
  1. Predator (Drone aircraft)–Juvenile literature. I. Title.
  UG1242.D7F56 2013
  623.74'69–dc23   2012007671

Printed in the United States of America, North Mankato, MN.

TABLE OF CONTENTS

PREDATOR DRONES

A Predator **drone** speeds through the sky. It is on a **mission** to find and destroy enemy weapons for the United States Air Force.

The **unmanned aerial vehicle (UAV)** searches the rocky desert below. Its cameras spot a large enemy gun.

Range ├┼┼┼┼┼┼┼┼┼┼┤
0   50   100

MISSILE

The Predator fires a **missile**. The enemy gun explodes in a ball of fire. Mission complete!

CREW, FEATURES, AND WEAPONS

PILOT

A **satellite** helps the crew operate the Predator from thousands of miles away. A pilot flies the Predator. A **sensor operator** controls the cameras and weapons.

Predator Fact

A mission coordinator sometimes works with the crew on complex missions.

The Predator usually flies about 85 miles (137 kilometers) per hour. This is not fast enough to appear on enemy **radar**.

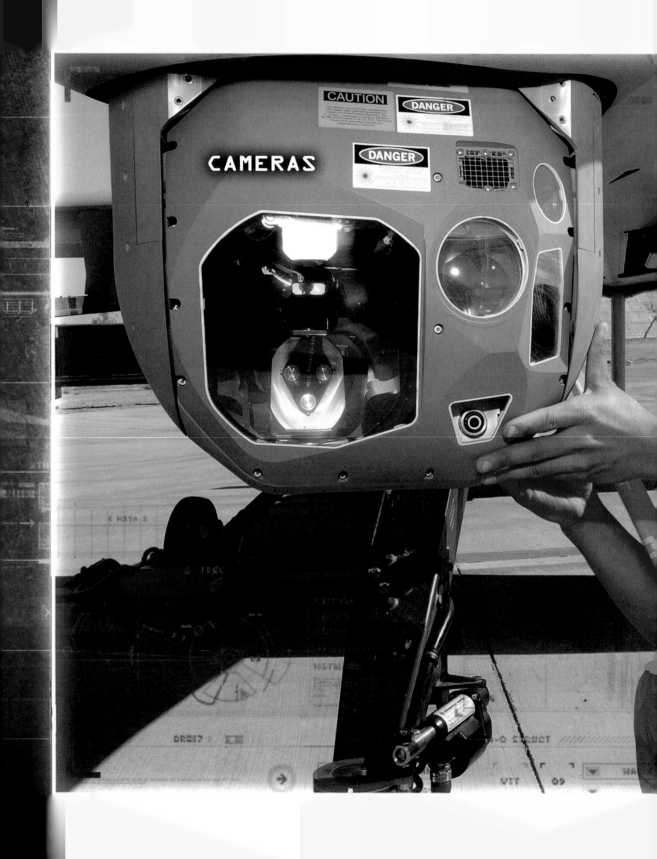

The Predator has special cameras and radar. These tools locate targets. **Lasers** help guide the Predator's missiles.

The Predator has a small engine. It is quiet and powerful. It can keep the Predator in the air for 24 hours!

Level

Latitude > 44°

Longitude > 20°

PREDATOR DRONE MISSIONS

Predators fly **recon** and **air support** missions. They have been used in the **War on Terror**.

Predator Fact

Predators can be taken apart. This makes them easy to transport.

VEHICLE BREAKDOWN: MQ-1B PREDATOR DRONE

Used By:	U.S. Air Force
Entered Service:	1995; missiles added in 2002
Length:	27 feet (8.2 meters)
Wingspan:	55 feet (16.8 meters)
Height:	6.9 feet (2.1 meters)
Weight (Fully Loaded):	2,250 pounds (1,020 kilograms)
Top Speed:	135 miles (217 kilometers) per hour
Range:	770 miles (1,240 kilometers)
Ceiling:	25,000 feet (7,620 meters)
Crew:	2 (not on board)
Weapons:	missiles
Primary Missions:	armed recon, air support

Speed

Range

0   50

Predator crews stay safe far away from the battlefield. They save the lives of soldiers with every weapon they destroy.

GLOSSARY

air support—a type of mission that involves flying close to and protecting soldiers on the ground

drone—an unmanned vehicle flown by remote control

lasers—small but intense beams of light

missile—an explosive that is guided to a target

mission—a military task

radar—a system that uses radio waves to locate targets

recon—a type of mission that involves gathering information about the enemy

satellite—an unmanned spacecraft that receives and sends radio signals

sensor operator—the crew member in charge of a Predator's cameras, radar, and weapons

unmanned aerial vehicle (UAV)—an airplane with no pilot inside; unmanned aerial vehicles are flown by remote control.

War on Terror—a conflict that began in 2001; the War on Terror has been fought in Afghanistan, Pakistan, and Iraq.

TO LEARN MORE

At the Library

David, Jack. *Predator Drones*. Minneapolis, Minn.:
Bellwether Media, 2008.

Fridell, Ron. *Military Technology*. Minneapolis, Minn.:
Lerner Publications Co., 2008.

Goldish, Meish. *Air Force: Civilian to Airman*. New York,
N.Y.: Bearport Pub., 2011.

On the Web

Learning more about Predator drones
is as easy as 1, 2, 3.

1. Go to www.factsurfer.com.

2. Enter "Predator drones" into the search box.

3. Click the "Surf" button and you will see a list
of related Web sites.

With factsurfer.com, finding more information
is just a click away.

INDEX